RUTHANNE TUDBALL

CLAY IN THE PRIMARY SCHOOL

CLAY IN THE PRIMARY SCHOOL

Warren Farnworth

B T BATSFORD LIMITED   LONDON

© Warren Farnworth 1973
First published 1973
ISBN 0 7134 2323 4

Designed by Charlotte Baron, Libra Studios
Filmset in Monophoto Bembo (270) 11 on 12 point by
Servis Filmsetting Limited, Manchester
Printed in Great Britain by William Clowes and Sons
Limited, Beccles, Suffolk
for the publishers
B T Batsford Limited
4 Fitzhardinge Street, London W1H 0AH

CONTENTS

Acknowledgment		5
1	Using Clay	7
2	Clay	14
	What is clay?	14
	Where to obtain it	15
	Digging and preparing your own clay	16
	Storage	18
	Handling	19
	Plasticity	22
	Clay slips	22
	Clays and firing	23
3	Pinch Techniques	26
	Cracking	29
	Thickness	29
	Shape	29
4	Coil Techniques	34
5	Slab Techniques	43
	Concave moulds	52
	Convex moulds	55
6	Modelling	62
7	Decoration	77
	Impressing	84
	Applied	91
	Incised	96
	Carving	99
	Inlay	101
	Painted	103
	Sgraffito	106
	Slip decorations	109
8	Kilns and Firing	115
	Kilns and firing	117
	Glazes and colourants	123
Bibliography		127
Suppliers		128

ACKNOWLEDGMENT

I should like to acknowledge the kind assistance of Mr K M Allan and his pupils at the Ellesmere County Primary School, Shropshire, and the following for permission to reproduce illustrations:
British Museum, London for figures 94, 124, 125, 127 and 180; Victoria and Albert Museum, London for figures 56, 96, 101, 116, 123, 139, 163, 186, 187, 189 and 192; the Cleveland Museum of Art, Ohio for figure 184; Gulbenkian Museum of Oriental Art, University of Durham for figure 155.
Jonathan Dytor ASTD, David Williams and Gareth Wyn Jones of the Denbighshire School of Art, Wrexham for figures 22–28, 42–53, 58, 77–89 and 159–162; Save the Children Fund for figures 1, 3 and 4; Camera Press for figure 2; Geremy Butler Photography for figures 30, 92 and 93; Fox Photos Limited for figure 109; Horniman Museum for figures 97 and 177; Mrs P Stemberg for figure 5.

Llangollen 1973   WF

Figure 2

Figure 1

1 USING CLAY

The approach to the use of clay in school is determined by so many factors, (the age of the children, the facilities available, the time to be spent, etc), that any recipe for learning will be in the nature of a tentative outline, rather than an inflexible dogma.

There is no logical reason for supposing that only the top juniors are old enough to attempt a coil pot, or that one must make a pinch pot before 'progressing' to a slab pot. There might sometimes be, and often are, good practical reasons for so doing, but they are only 'good' reasons inasmuch that they relate to a given class of children, with a given teacher, at a given time.

The material itself provides its own logic, and cultivates its own discipline. Those who have used clay themselves, attempted to shape it this way and that, will know what I mean. However ambitious one's first intention, one is soon caught up, not in a one-sided conversation, (telling the clay what to do), but in a dialogue, listening, responding, feeling one's way into a situation where what happens, how it happens, and why it happens, assume real significance.

A climate which enables children to partake of similar experiences at their own level, (and with a five-year-old, this is exactly the kind of intimate experience which we often do see taking place), is the kind of climate which we should all strive to achieve.

To ask how one achieves it is a leading question. Surely no-one can expect the answer to lie in some magical list of 'do's and 'don't's. Do's and don'ts there may be, (in terms of the technical handling of clay, there are a great many of them), but added together, they do not provide us with all the necessary and sufficient conditions.

Parts of the answer will, I hope, suggest themselves in the pages which follow, when we consider in more detail how clay can be used, and how clay has been used in the past; for much that is true about one's honest dealings with clay, is equally true about one's honest dealings with children.

To meet clay for the first time is a unique experience. Whether one is five or fifty-five, there is an almost uncontrollable urge to poke it, pull it, press it, touch it.

The urge may wear off for different reasons at different times. Some people never tire of it; for others, it makes them sneeze. Children sometimes reject it because it is 'dirty'; others because they can't think what to do with it; and still others because it is frustrating. Most children continue to enjoy using it because they can make it do what they want. They like the feel of it. It's nice to play with.

This easy affinity with a natural material lies at the heart of using clay. It is something to be nurtured and explored. It is the necessary first step in understanding about clay.

Figure 3

To begin with, this means providing opportunities for exploratory play at the child's own level, in much the same way that we encourage free play with sand or water.

However undisciplined it might appear, a good deal of real learning is taking place. Learning about the properties of clay; learning how it reacts when it is used in different ways; developing skill in the use of hands, tools and so on. The teacher's most difficult task is to stand back rather than be too overtly involved in what the children do and how they do it.

Little is gained from imposing adult stands of form and technique too early. These (particularly with infants) can and will develop naturally, if the teacher provides the kind of situation where clay can be progressively explored.

First encourage the manipulation of clay with hands and fingers. Most children do this naturally, for clay shouts out to be pressed and poked, rolled and patted, pulled and stretched, squashed and pinched. But nevertheless, these are vital activities to be borne in mind, and actively to be introduced and discussed.

Secondly, provide opportunities for using clay in its various states. Obviously, much of the children's work will be carried out using plastic clay, but here and there, one might introduce clay in its 'cheese-hard' state, (an excellent consistency for cutting and carving); clay in its dry state, (providing opportunities for scraping, scoring, sawing, chipping, and breaking); and even, (if a corner to be messy in is available), clay in its liquid state, providing opportunities for pouring and mixing.

Figure 4   Using cheese-hard clay

Thirdly, encourage the use of tools. This is not a signal to go out and buy an expensive collection of boxwood modelling tools and clay cutters, but to make judicious use of all kinds of odds and ends which are freely available. Matchsticks, lollipop sticks, old brush handles, pieces of wood, etc. Old table knives, spoons, broken plastic scissors, nail files, and pieces of metal. Empty bottles and containers, pastry cutters, bottle tops, corks, pieces of wire, screws and nails, and so on. The list is endless.

It would certainly be useful to have a collection, or rather a number of collections of odds and ends like these, kept in boxes, and made freely available for use. Initially, their use might be limited. First providing things which can be stuck into clay; seeds, buttons, matchsticks, etc. Next, providing things which can be used for cutting; knives, scissors, etc. Then introducing things which can be used for shaping, texturing, forming, rolling, and so on. Later on, these naturally developed skills will be of immense importance.

This early exploratory phase of clay-using is reflected in the objects which result.

Using the clay as a drawing medium; an understandable adaptation of clay to the prior habit of making a mark with crayon or pencil.

Shaping the form from a solid piece of clay by patting and pressing, before scoring and impressing the features of an owl.

Or shaping the form as an aggregate of large and small pieces, pushed and pressed together to describe an apprehensive cat.

Figure 5 *(above)* Sticking things into clay. *Porcupine*, boy aged 7

Figure 6 *(below)* Tools for cutting and shaping

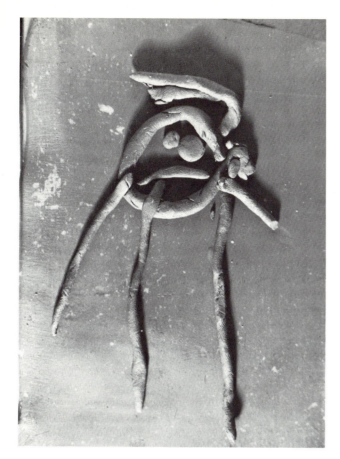

Figure 7 *(above left)*

Figure 8 *(above right)*

Figure 9 *(below right)*

Figure 10

Indeed, I often feel that young children very seldom surpass the honesty and directness which they achieve in their first clay models. Rather is the problem one of sustaining the child's natural inquisitiveness about clay, without engendering the whole process with an element of competitive precocity, where the first one to make a cottage-shaped teapot is the winner.

Two factors would seem to be involved. Firstly, the child's growing concern with ideas rather than with materials. A young child will contentedly play with clay because he is interested in the material itself; eager to experiment with it, and to find out how it responds when used in different ways. An older child will see clay as a medium which can be used to express an idea, whether it be of a prehistoric monster or an ashtray for father. It is the difference between the young child's, 'Let me play with it', and the older one's, 'What shall I make?'

The second factor is the child's growing awareness of adult standards. The inevitable realisation that clay is not just something which you play with at school, but is the same material which was used to make mother's precious Spode teapot, or Aunt Maud's Dresden doll, must come as a sobering thought. It must certainly have shattered many illusions about the worth of one's own, rather crude terra-cotta dragon.

Clay, surmise many children, is child's play, unless it can be used to approximate more nearly to the pots which adults use, and seem to cherish.

For the primary school teacher, both these factors present difficulties of a very real kind. The former demands that new ideas, approaches and techniques be judiciously introduced. The latter demands a sensitive appraisal of what kinds of new ideas, etc, are introduced, and how, when and why they are introduced.

It would be a simple ploy, for instance, when faced with a waning interest in the use of clay, to introduce the use of commercially-made plaster moulds. Plaster moulds of all kinds are readily available, and are com-

The decision to introduce new techniques, and to develop new skills, is very much to be made by the teacher on the spot. Some children seem content to use clay in their own way without outside assistance and advice, for a long period. Others soon want to put away childish things and proceed to something new, or more complicated.

It would be wrong to suppose that simple 'hand modelling' was a kind of first step, to be got over as soon as possible, before the real work of pottery began.

paratively easy to use, even for very young children. The ease with which one can reproduce a clay casting of a Disneyesque rabbit, or a late Victorian styled vase, is quite remarkable. It demands little effort and little skill. Some children love it. Needless to say, in half a term or so, interest will wane again. We might sustain the child's interest by providing bigger and better moulds, or by introducing some other gratuitous trick. (For make no mistake, trickery it is, and of the worst kind.) But what then? Even were it conceivable to carry on the charade of interest until the age of eleven, what would have been achieved? Practically nothing, other than warping whatever appreciation might otherwise have developed.

Although the child's interest must clearly be sustained, it must not be sustained at the expense of all else. The fact that children need the challenge which the mastering of a new technique presents; need the sense of achievement which the acquisition of a new skill brings; and need the motivation for action which a new stimulus promotes, must go hand in hand with the conviction that some things are worthy, and others are not; that some things are important, and others trivial; and that children should begin to know the truth of this.

The child's natural inquisitiveness is a wonderful gift. This infant's clay dog stems from his inquisitiveness about clay, rather than about dogs. The idea of making a dog was a consequence of his using clay, rather than a reason for it.

The older child's model of refugees, on the other hand, stems from an inquisitiveness about refugees. Clay is simply the medium through which his ideas are expressed. One might not unreasonably suggest that some of the poignancy of his representation stems from a real involvement with the subject of 'refugees', rather than with his preoccupation with clay. Whereas the infant might continue to use clay to fashion his dogs, or whatever else might occur to him, for a considerable period, (since this is a period of inquisitiveness about

Figure 11

clay, rather than the things which clay can represent), the older child's inquisitiveness about refugees might soon pass.

But another investigation will take its place. To sensibly relate this new inquisitiveness, (sensibly and not artificially), to the child's use of clay, is to provide a situation for learning which has point and purpose. New skills, new ideas, and new approaches are the constituents which give form to these new situations.

2 CLAY

WHAT IS CLAY?

The last time I asked this question of a class of junior school children, I found myself confronted with a sea of blank faces. What an odd question to ask, they must have thought; doesn't he know? Surely, even a teacher must know what clay is. Some of them, obviously impressed with the apparent seriousness of the question, searched their minds for the semblance of an answer. 'Mud' 'Soil' 'Dirt'.

Others were completely non-plussed, and ignored the question as an irrelevance. Clay is clay, and that's that.

For the most part, I will assume that we do in fact know what clay is, in the sense that we can recognise it when we see it, and rarely mistake it for peanut butter or putty.

Although it might sometimes be helpful to know that clay is formed by the gradual decomposition of certain granite-type rocks, in much the same way that sand is formed by the erosion of sandstone, we are hardly wiser by learning that clay is an impure hydrated silicate of aluminium. Those who wish to pursue the topic further, in a more scientific way, must refer to some of the books listed in the bibliography.

WHERE TO OBTAIN IT

The easiest way is to buy it direct from a pottery supplier, some of which are listed at the end of the book. Almost certainly they will have prepared the clay for themselves, and will be familiar with its advantages and disadvantages, and if things do go wrong, they will be always willing to help and advise. Indeed, if you happen to live near the supplier, the company will usually be quite happy to show you and the children how the clay has been prepared. For those who are unable to dig the clay for themselves, such a visit would help the children to associate the clean, plastic modelling clay which the teacher gives them from a polythene bag, with the 'messy mud' at the bottom of the garden.

At first sight, the catalogue of a pottery supplier can be rather daunting. It isn't just a case of 'clay' at so much per kilogram (pound). Generally, a dozen or so different kinds of clay will be listed, to be purchased, rather macabrely, as dry bodies or prepared bodies.

But take heart. Remember that your supplier will doubtless be supplying clay to all kinds of people, from studio potters to teachers in colleges of art. Clay, for them, is very important. For us it is far less so. We can in fact make do with the cheapest clay on the list. This would be listed as 'modelling clay' or 'earthenware'. But if you still feel unsure, the suppliers themselves would advise you on the most suitable clay for work in the primary school.

In choosing the clay, two points should be borne in mind. Firstly the colour of the clay. The colour referred to in the catalogue, is the colour which the clay will be after firing. Red clay isn't red, it's usually a chocolate brown. Only after firing would it take on a reddish-orange colour. White clay might be white or pale grey, whereas buff clay would be buff, whether fired or not. To all intents and purposes, it matters little whichever colour you buy. For modelling in the classroom, one colour would be just as good as any other, the only (major) difference being that red clay contains iron oxide, and white or grey clay doesn't.

The advantage of white or grey clay is that it is slightly cleaner to use; and when dry, gives you a lighter surface on which to paint with powder colour or oxide. The advantage of red clay is that, for children, it looks more like clay.

The second point to remember is the state of the clay. Plastic or prepared bodies are clays which are ready for use; not too hard, not too soft. Dry bodies are clays in powder form, which require mixing with water before they are usable.

Always buy the plastic, never the dry. In theory, although it requires only to be mixed with water, in practice it involves hours of quite unnecessary toil and will never be one half as good as the plastic clay which you should have bought in the first place.

Assuming that the clay will be used over and over again, fifty kilos would suffice for an average-sized class, using it about twice a week, for nearly a whole term. If you intend to let the children keep everything which they make, it will last about two to three weeks. On average therefore, I would recommend about two to three fifty kilo bags per term.

Figure 12

DIGGING AND PREPARING YOUR OWN CLAY

Before we consider what to do with the clay when it arrives, let's consider the alternative of digging the clay oneself. Clearly, there are advantages and disadvantages. The most that teachers can do is to weigh the ones against the others, and decide for themselves.

I would propose two advantages. Firstly, the sheer, physical enjoyment of 'messing about' with clay. Looking for it, finding it, digging it, mixing it, and preparing it. Secondly, the understanding which it engenders. In a very real sense, one can never fully appreciate, never fully respond to clay as a medium, certainly never draw in one's breath with admiration when we see an Aztec pot or a neolithic bowl, until and unless we have dug our own hands into raw material, and transformed it from crude earth to fashionable clay. Those who might gasp in admiration at a neolithic pot without first so doing, would gasp even more if they did. To meet clay always halfway, as something out of a plastic bag, pure and antiseptic, is to deny oneself and the children a substantial joy.

In a sense, there are no disadvantages. Digging and preparing one's own clay is never disadvantageous. It is the question of time, effort and know-how which present the problems. Given the time, many teachers would be prepared to do it, if they knew how. The clay thus obtained would be every bit as good as 'bought' clay, and would cost nothing.

Perhaps in practice, the wisest plan would be to try to give every child, at some point in time, the experience of digging and preparing his own clay, whilst relying on 'bought' clay for most of the modelling to be done in the classroom.

The first step is to find out where the clay can be dug. Some of you will be lucky enough to find it on your own doorstep, as it were, in the school garden or the playing field. You might have to dig for it; you might find it exposed on the surface. Others may have to go further afield. Local building sites are often likely sources, as are banks of ponds or streams. Some of you may even live near a local pottery or brick works, where plentiful supplies of high-quality clay can be readily obtained.

Figure 13

Some of you, alas, will just be unfortunate, living in an area where clay cannot be found. But if you do find it difficult to locate, have a chat with the local builder or borough surveyor. They should be able to tell you where to find it.

Having found it, it should be collected and brought back to school. Plastic carrier bags and garden trowels should suffice for this, and it doesn't matter whether the clay is hard, plastic, or sloppy. It can all be used.

The first stage in its preparation will depend on the nature of the clay itself. Some clays can be dug and used right away, without any further treatment. Others, because they are too hard or too soft, or because they are full of impurities, (stones, soil, vegetable matter, etc), have to be specially prepared.

Let's assume that your clay is hard and full of impurities. This is the sequence of operations.
1 Allow the clay to dry out completely.
2 When dry, break up the clay into small pieces, (about the size of a walnut).
3 Soak the dry pieces of clay in a bucket of water. In point of fact, it doesn't matter what you soak it in, but a bucketful is a manageable quantity.
4 Allow the clay to soak until it has broken down into a thick slop. This is a potter's term meaning exactly what it sounds like. It will take about one or two days, after which time, the slop will lie as a sediment at the bottom of the bucket, the water on the top.

Figure 14

5 Mix the clay and the water in the bucket to make a fairly thin slop. This can now be sieved. All you require is a second bucket, (for sieving into), and a sieve. A fine garden sieve will do, or, (but more time-consuming), a metal kitchen sieve. A good, stiff brush is useful to pass the clay through the sieve, but willing hands are equally efficacious. This will rid the clay of most of the unwanted impurities.

6 Again, allow the slop to settle. As it settles, the water can gradually be poured off, leaving the thickening clay at the bottom. In practice, were you to leave the clay for a couple of weeks or so, it would gradually dry out naturally by evaporation, to the point where it was of ideal consistency for modelling. Indeed, for the busy teacher, this might be the best thing to do. If, however, you need the clay rather more urgently, it can be dried relatively quickly by spreading it out onto an old sack in the school playground.

STORAGE

Once the clay has reached the desired consistency, it must be carefully stored. Here we can return to the point where we left the 'bought' clay. The clay which arrives in school, well-wrapped in plastic bags or polythene sheets, and the clay which we have prepared for ourselves, should now be in perfect condition; not so soft that it sticks to the hand, nor so hard that it is unresponsive to the touch. In theory, either clay, if kept under the right conditions, will retain this usable state indefinitely. In practice, this means keeping the clay free from contact with the air. It is vitally important to realise that as soon as clay is exposed to air, particularly in conjunction with warm, eager hands, it begins to harden, and will continue to harden to the point when it is completely unworkable.

Depending on the quantity to be stored, any container with a close-fitting lid would be adequate, (biscuit tins, dustbins, buckets, etc). Plastic ones are more suitable than metal ones, since the latter soon rusts, although rust itself has no harmful effect. To be absolutely sure, (since lids are rarely completely airtight), cover the clay with a sheet of polythene, or a damp sack, and check it frequently. If no containers are available, keep the clay tightly wrapped in a polythene sheet.

Storage of work in progress
If it is not possible for the children to complete their clay models in one lesson, care must be taken to store the unfinished work in an airtight container to prevent the clay from hardening. Polythene bags or sheets, wrapped securely around the work, are quite adequate for this, and will keep the clay in a soft, plastic state for many months.

HANDLING

Next we must consider some of the problems involved in actually using the clay. Firstly, the condition of the clay. The main difference between our two clays, the bought clay and the prepared clay, can be seen simply by looking at it.

The bought clay is in one homogeneous piece. If we cut it in half with a cheese wire, we can see its close, even texture, free from lumps and air-pockets.

The prepared clay, on the other hand, (assuming we have simply collected it and rolled it together after drying it on a sack), will be lumpy, bitty, and full of holes.

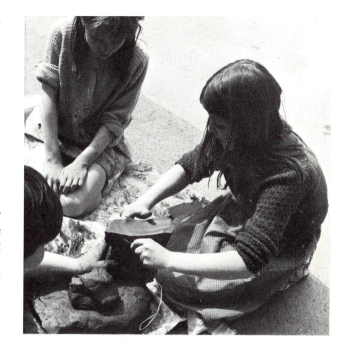

Figure 15 *(above)*

Figure 16 *(below)*

In terms of most of the work to be done in the primary school, and irrespective of what the purists might say, either clay could be given out and used immediately. Strictly speaking, it is only when clay articles are intended for firing in a kiln, that we need worry about wedging and kneading, and I will say more about this later.

Secondly, distribution. Simply cut up the clay into desired-size pieces and give it out. Tearing at the clay with your hands can be rather difficult, so use a length of wire or strong, nylon thread (wound round a wooden handle at either end), cutting through the clay as the grocer cuts through cheese.

When all is completed, return the unused clay to the store, or leave it on a desk, well-covered with a polythene sheet or damp cloth. Never leave it exposed to the air and insist that the children too keep the clay well-covered.

The third problem, perhaps the hardest, is that of collecting the clay. Some of it will have been legitimately used up, in the making of models and pots and so on, but a good deal more will be left behind on the modelling boards, not to mention the bits on the floor. Some of the residue may still be soft and usable, in which case it can be returned to the storage bin, and used again. But most of it will be in hard bits and pieces.

This unusuable residue must be collected in a separate bucket or bin and covered with water. Left for two to three days, the pieces will break down into a thick slop, to be reconstituted as we described earlier.

In theory, therefore, the procedure for clay storage and usage is quite simple. One bin contains good, usable clay; another contains slop. As the slop thickens, or is dried out on sacks, it can be returned to the usable bin.

However, more often than not, one of three things will occur, (discounting the horrid thought that all three things might happen together).

1 Slop will accumulate and stores of good, usable clay will decrease. Here, the remedy is simple, if arduous. One declares war on the slop, making a concerted effort to dry it out, whenever and wherever possible.

2 Types of clay will multiply. Maybe you have taken over a new class, or changed your clay supplier, to find yourself with one bin of red clay, one bin of white, and one bin of assorted odds and ends. If that happens, ignore it. You can mix the differently coloured clays together without any ill effects. Here again, purists might disagree. They would have us keep a multitude of bins, one for each colour, with an edict against ever mixing them together. Inasmuch that it is sometimes useful to have a red clay and a white clay, I would agree with them. But given the existing conditions in most primary schools; given the fact that the classroom teacher just hasn't the time to spend in sorting out one clay from the next; and given that a 'mixed' clay is no whit inferior to an 'unmixed' one, I would again say, ignore it.

3 Most calamitous of all, your stock of good, usable clay will dry out. It happens in the best-ordered circles. Someone forgets to replace the dustbin lid; the clay is left unattended during the school holidays; or the airtight plastic bag has a hole in it.

Whatever the cause, the clay must be reclaimed. The method of reclamation depends both on the degree of hardness which the clay has reached and the amount of time and help which is available.

By *degree of hardness* I refer to the clay being in a state which potters describe as *cheese-* or *leather-hard,* where the clay has the texture of firm cheese, too hard to model with, yet capable of being cut with a wire; or in a state where the clay is almost completely dry. In future, I will refer to these states as *cheese-hard* or *dry*.

The simplest method is to break up the clay into small pieces, soak it in water to obtain a thick slop and dry out as described above. Cheese-hard clay can be broken up by using a wire, (cutting it into thick slices), or a spoon, (digging it out piece by piece). Dry clay should be crushed with a hammer or brick.

The other method can only be used for cheese-hard clay. Cut the clay into thin slices with a wire and make a sandwich of alternate layers of clay and slop. Re-slice the whole sandwich across the grain and continue slicing until the cheese-hard clay and the slop are well mixed together. Finish by kneading the clay (as you would dough), until the mixture is of workable consistency.

If the clay is still too soft, use more cheese-hard clay. Although the process sounds rather difficult and indeed it is to begin with, with practice, a bucket-sized quantity of clay can be reclaimed in less than half-an-hour. The obvious advantage of this method is that usable clay can be made from cheese-hard clay and slop, without the necessity of drying-out, watering-down, and drying-out again.

Figure 17 *(above)*

Figure 18 *(below)*

PLASTICITY

Clays are of many kinds. Some are referred to as being highly plastic, others less so. A potter might use the terms *short* and *fat,* and the obvious analogy with short and fat pastry is a very close one. Short clays, like short pastry, are crumbly, difficult to work, and prone to excessive cracking. Fat clays are responsive to the touch, easily workable, and far less prone to cracking.

Bought clays have been so prepared that their plasticity is about right, being neither too short, nor too fat; and since teachers will tend to use bought clay almost exclusively, problems of plasticity will rarely arise. However, even with bought clays, a loss of plasticity can be induced. If they are repeatedly dried out, watered-down into slop, and reconstituted, the level of plasticity will decrease. With prepared clays dug from the school garden, the problem may be more pronounced. The plasticity of many local clays is so low as to make them virtually unworkable. Fortunately, the remedy is simple enough. If clay is too short, mix it with a quantity of new, bought clay, making a sandwich of alternate layers of the two clays, and knead them together.

CLAY SLIPS

Slip is clay in liquid form; a refined slop. It is made by soaking small pieces of clay in water, until the clay turns to slop. The slop should be sieved. Specially-made sieves are available from pottery suppliers, varying in size from 10 mesh to 200 mesh. The size refers to the fineness of the mesh; 10 being fairly coarse, 200 being very fine. For slip sieving, an 80 or 100 mesh sieve should be used.

For general use, (see chapter 7) slip should be the consistency of double cream. The colour of the slip will naturally depend on the colour of the clay from which it is made, but it can be coloured artificially by using oxides, (if the finished article is to be fired), or powder paint, coloured ink, or dyes. Oxide colourants are referred to in chapter 8.

CLAYS AND FIRING

Lastly, a word about clay and firing. Many people give the impression that unless clay articles are to be fired in a kiln, the whole activity of using clay loses its relevance. I disagree.

For many teachers in the primary school, the firing of clay is simply not possible. Even if it were, no one could seriously suggest that it was the vital culmination of every creative activity period in which infants had been given the opportunity of 'playing' with clay. The plain fact is that although there are times when it is desirable that a child's effort be properly fired and glazed, there are many other times when it matters not one way or the other. One might hope that at some point in their primary schooling, children might be given the opportunity to experience something of the magic of the firing process, and to have some of their own pots and models fired in a pottery kiln, but it would be too idealistic to imagine that everything which they ever made from clay would, could, or even should be fired. However, since this chapter is concerned with clay, and since, later on, we will discuss some of the methods by which the primary school teacher might build a simple kiln, and conduct a simple firing with the children, we will consider some of the special precautions which must be taken.

Two factors must be borne in mind. Firstly, that when clay is heated it contracts. Secondly, and this applies particularly to clays which are to be fired in a simple bonfire or sawdust kiln, it must be able to withstand sudden changes in temperature.

At first glance, one clay model might look exactly like another, yet one might explode in the firing, the other will remain intact. Why? Almost inevitably, because the exploded model contained hidden pockets of air, and the intact one did not. During the firing, the trapped air would expand, the clay would contract, and the model would explode. In other words, clay which is to be fired must be free from pockets of air. To ensure this, the clay is wedged and kneaded. In practice, clay which is used directly from a newly-opened bag of bought clay can usually be safely used without this. All other clays, particularly amalgams of odds and ends of clay of varying consistency, or prepared clays, must be treated.

Wedging
Cutting a large slab of clay into thick slices, slapping them down very hard together in a different order, and repeating the process ten to twenty times.

Kneading
This is done with the hands in roughly the same way that one would knead dough. Using the base of the palm of the hands, press downwards into the clay, forcing it away from the body.

Lift up the furthest edge of the clay, bringing it over and back towards the body, and press down again with the palms of the hands.

The effect of this rhythmic pressing down and pulling back, should be to fashion the clay into the shape of an ox head.

Clay which is sufficiently kneaded should, when cut in two with a wire, exhibit a close, even, air-pocket-free surface, like the clay in figure 15.

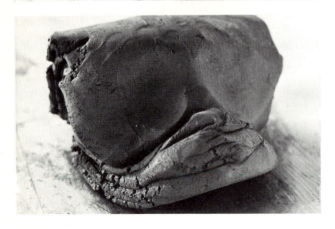

Figure 19 *(above)*

Figure 20 *(centre)*

Figure 21 *(below)*

Clay which is eventually to be fired in some kind of primitive kiln, where models are often exposed to rapid changes in temperature, must be strengthened or 'opened' with sand or grog. The term *grog* refers to clay which has been fired and broken down into coarse granules or powder. This can be obtained from a pottery supplier. Sand, (almost any kind will do), is cheaper, and equally effective.

To mix the clay and sand (or grog) together, cut the clay into slices; make a sandwich of alternate layers of sand and clay, and knead them together. Since both sand or grog have the effect of drying out the clay, it is advisable to use clay which is slightly softer than clay used for modelling. If this is not available, intersperse each slice of clay with a thin layer of slop.

Proportions of clay to sand are not critical, although sand will decrease the level of plasticity, and 2 to 3 parts clay to 1 of sand should prove adequate. Apart from its superior strength and coarse texture, grogged or sanded clay is no different from, and can be used in exactly the same way as other clays. If necessary, ungrogged and grogged clays can happily be mixed together.

Those who wish to experiment further with textured clays, can try out admixtures of sawdust, grass seed, chopped grass cuttings, iron filings, etc. None of these substances will make the clay stronger, but they will produce interesting surface effects, whether fired or not.

3 PINCH TECHNIQUES

An infant will make the semblance of a pinch pot, (some people refer to them as thumb pots), in a few minutes. To make a good one might take a lifetime. The shorter method is as follows.

Take a piece of clay about the size of a small apple, and shape it in the hands, as one shapes a snowball, until you have a smooth sphere. With the ball of clay cradled in the palm of your hand, press the thumb of the other hand into the centre of the ball to make a deep hole. This gives the start of a thick-walled pot. Still cradling the clay in the palm of your hand, pinch out the wall of the pot between fingers and thumb; the thumb on the inside, the fingers on the outside.

The pinching-out process is a gradual one. Don't try to pinch out the wall of the pot to the desired thickness in one go. Ease the clay gently, bit by bit. Since each pinch thins out only a section of the wall, the pot is slowly rotated in the palm of the hand. Pinch the wall, turn the pot in the hand. Pinch and turn, pinch and turn.

With practise, you will develop a rhythm. A smooth, reassuring rhythm, which gives the pot its simple, symmetrical form.

Figure 22 *(opposite above left)*

Figure 23 *(opposite above right)*

Figure 24 *(opposite below left)*

Figure 25 *(opposite below right)*

Figure 26 *(above left)*

Figure 27 *(above right)*

Figure 28 *(below left)*

A similar kind of technique can be used to press out any kind of shape, resting the clay on a board, rather than in the hand. Although children find this an easier method to master, it lacks the intimacy which traditional pinch pot making has, and, (since the base of the pot is inevitably pressed out flat), it never achieves a comparable grace of form.

Figure 29 *(above)*

Figure 30 *(below)*   Two pinched forms by Mary Rogers. Very thinly pinched clay which grows naturally into flower-like and petal-like shapes

CRACKING

This is the most common difficulty experienced when making a traditional pinch pot; resulting from the use of too-hard a clay, or prolonged handling. Smooth over the emerging cracks with a moist finger or damp sponge, as soon as they appear. Be careful not to over-wet the pot. If the clay becomes too dry, and the cracks very severe, the best policy is to start again with a new piece of clay.

THICKNESS

The right thickness for the wall of the pot depends on a number of factors. The size of the pot, the age and experience of the child, the clay being used, and so on. To begin with, keep the walls of the pot fairly thick, particularly around the rim. Later, with practice, you can begin to experiment with very thinly pinched shapes.

SHAPE

By all means experiment with the various ways in which hands and clay can be used together, creating shallow bowls with the palm fully open; or thin, tube-like shapes with the palm pulled together. But do strive to work consciously *with* the clay, rather than dishonestly forcing it into some pre-conceived notion of a Sévres vase or a modern tea-cup.

Once this basic technique is mastered, we are ready to exploit it, sensitively and creatively.

Figure 31 *(above left)* Other clay shapes have been added to the basic pinch pot to create a simple bird

Figure 32 *(above right)*

Figure 33 *(below right)*

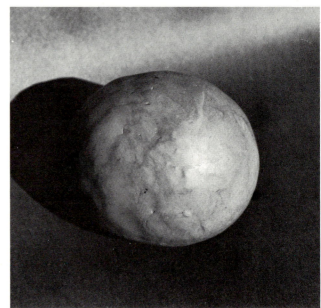

By fastening two pinch pots together, rim to rim, we can make a simple pebble form. Fasten them by scoring the two lips, brushing over with thick slip and pressing hard together, see page 57. Smooth over the outside join with fingers or a modelling tool. This is an important technique which can be used in a variety of ways. Compared with a similarly shaped solid piece of clay, it has two obvious advantages. Firstly, it uses less clay, (hence making it lighter and cheaper); secondly, it can be more successfully fired.

Figure 34   Simple pierced and cut shapes, made from a double pinch pot shape

Figure 35

Figure 36   Lipped, pinched forms by Leslie Cameron

By cutting a hole in the top pinch pot, and pinching-out the rim, we can make a simple pot. This has been impressed with the end of a modelling tool. If we think of these simple pots, lying on their side, we can see how, by adding legs and a nose, or scales, etc, the shape can be developed into almost anything, from a piggy-bank to a strange fish.

Figure 37 *(opposite above left)*

Figure 38 *(opposite above right)*

Figure 39 *(opposite below left)*   Chris Sansome

Figure 40 *(opposite below right)*   By using more than two pinch pots together, all manner of shapes can be developed. Chris Sansome

4 COIL TECHNIQUES

Figure 41 Earthenware jar with impressed decoration. Chinese, third century BC. Ashmolean Museum, Oxford

No two people will make a coil pot in exactly the same way. Each will adapt the fundamentals of the technique to suit his own individual way of working. To insist, therefore, that children slavishly adopt one's own arbitrary and idiosyncratic technique is to be too dogmatic and constricting. Much of the beauty of a well-made coil pot results from the rhythmic union of a man and his clay. The rhythm is important. The sense of union is important. Technical considerations apart, how one makes the coils, and fastens them together, is not.

The natural way to make a coil is by rolling the clay beneath one's fingers. It is a deceptively simple technique, for to make a long coil of even thickness, demands much practise. The secret would seem to lie in the rhythm of one's body, rolling the clay backwards and forwards, pressing down and easing out the clay with the fingers, whilst the clay is in motion. Pressing down when the clay is still results in a flattening of the coil from a circular section to an oval one. It is not essential that the coils be of even size and thickness, nor should one necessarily insist upon it. It is merely rewarding to feel that one has mastered the skill, and that one can draw on it if necessary. For the beginner, keep the coils fairly thick. For a small, cup-sized pot, the coils should be about as thick as a fountain pen; certainly no thinner. Making the coils too thin is a beginner's most common failing.

If the clay is soft, make about five or six coils before you begin, allowing them time to firm up. If the clay is sufficiently firm to begin with, make the coils singly, as and when required.

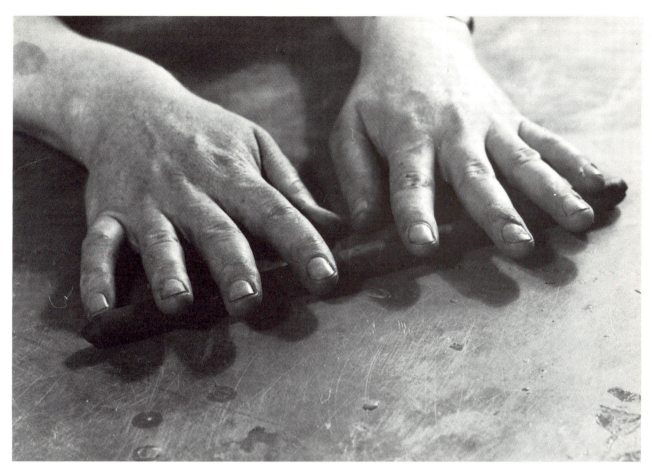

Figure 42

For the base of the pot, flatten out a ball of clay into a flat disc, about the same thickness as the coils. Now coiling can begin.

Take the first coil and shape it around the inside edge of the base, pressing the inside edge of the coil firmly down onto the base. When the coil comes full circle, continue around on top of the first coil, pressing this coil firmly down, by smearing the inside edge down onto the coil beneath.

This basic action is continued, coil by coil, until the pot is completed, the shape of the pot being largely determined by the placing of the coils. If the pot is to swell out, coils must be placed on the outer circumference of the coil beneath. If the pot is to become narrower, coils must be placed on the inside circumference.

Many potters suggest that pots should be built up from separate rings of clay, with the two ends of each coil being fastened together on the completion of each full circle. Apart from giving the pot a slightly more regular pattern of coils, this method offers no advantages, and is slower in execution. Some would go so far as to insist that the join between each coil should be scored and painted with slip. Assuming that the clay is of the correct consistency, (soft enough for two coils to be securely bonded together by smearing the one down onto the other), this practice too is over-cautious and time-wasting. If the clay is so hard that it really does need this treatment, it is arguably too hard for children to use anyway.

Figure 47

Figure 43 (*opposite above left*)

Figure 44 (*opposite above right*)

Figure 45 (*opposite below left*)   Outer coils joined with modelling tool

Figure 46 (*opposite below right*)   The partly smoothed-over pot

A pot, the height of six to ten coils, can be made in one session. A larger one might take three or more sessions, allowing time between each session for the clay to firm up, otherwise it would begin to sag, the soft coils at the bottom being unable to bear the weight of the coils above. Judging when to rest the pot and when to continue is an important skill which takes time to acquire.

Rest the pot immediately it shows signs of loosing shape. It usually takes an hour to firm sufficiently for new coils to be added. Since this usually means that the pot has to be stored until the child's next lesson, care must be taken not to let the pot become too hard, or remain too soft.

Figure 48

When a new session of coiling begins, the clay must be just right. Not too soft that the pot begins to sag after putting on the first coil; nor too hard that there is a marked difference in consistency between the old coils and the new. If the pot has over-hardened, the top coil must be gradually softened down by scoring and brushing with thick slip, until its consistency is that of the new coil to be added. Failure to do this will result in cracking when the finished pot gradually dries out.

Two further techniques might be mentioned here, since, in execution, they are very similar to coiling. Firstly, that of building up the pot, not from coils, but from lumps of clay of random shape and size. The clay should be of the same consistency, and should be joined together inside the pot by the same method of smearing the edges of one piece of clay over the pieces adjoining it.

Figure 49

Figure 50

39

Secondly, that of building up the pot from pellets of clay, which may or may not be of the same size. The advantage of this method is merely that it creates a distinctive form of surface decoration. In every other respect, it is the same as the one mentioned earlier.

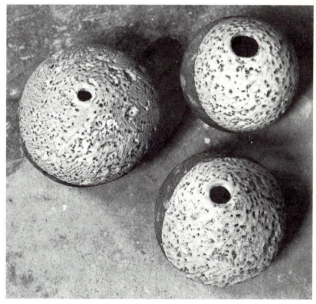

Figure 51 *(opposite above)*

Figure 52 *(opposite below left)*

Figure 53 *(opposite below right)*

Figure 54 *(above)*   A coiled bottle by a six-year-old

Figure 55 *(below)*   Three rounded coiled shapes. Grains of rice mixed with the clay before coiling, provide coarse-grained texture

Figure 56 Coiling can be used in all kinds of ways. A figure might be built up from a number of coiled sections, like this clay dog. Chinese, Han dynasty, Victoria and Albert Museum, Crown Copyright

Figure 57 Coiled figure

5 SLAB TECHNIQUES

The final, important, clay-working technique is that of slab-work, where the article is built up from slabs or sheets of clay. We can fashion a lump of clay into a flat slab by rolling out the clay with a rolling pin until we have the desired thickness.

To prevent the clay from sticking to the rolling surface, always roll it out on a piece of cloth or paper. Cloth (any kind will do) is preferable, since it can be used over and over again, but any kind of paper is equally efficacious.

For rolling out, wooden rolling pins are best, but on no account should they be bought specially for the occasion. Bottles, thick cardboard tubes, sawn-up broom handles, pieces of metal piping, are all equally usable. To ensure an even thickness of slab (if this is desirable), two sticks placed on either side of the clay, of equal thickness can be used as a rest for the rolling pin. Ideally, clay for rolling-out should be slightly, (only slightly) firmer than that used for coiling or pinch work. If the clay is too soft, and sticks to the rolling pin, wipe the rolling pin with a damp cloth, and roll out the clay more gently. Better still, allow the clay time to harden slightly.

Figure 58

Young children could well dispense with the rolling pin and the sticks and press out the clay on a piece of paper with their hands.

With a slab of clay, we can do all manner of things. We may make a tile, cutting the shape with a knife or a pastry cutter. Older children can make their own cutters from a piece of stiff card or tin.

Using a number of tiles together, we can make a tile panel, or cut the clay very small to make a mosaic.

Figure 59 *(opposite above left)* We may use the clay as a surface on which to draw or impress a picture

Figure 60 *(opposite above right)*

Figure 61 *(opposite below left)*

Figure 62 *(opposite below right)*

Figure 63

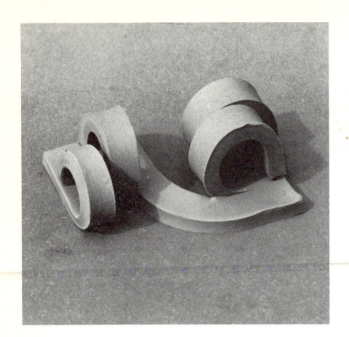
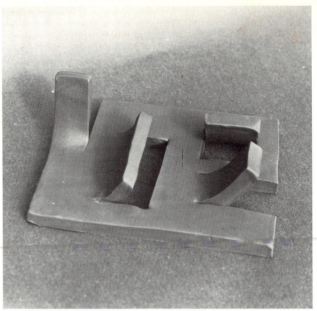

By cutting, bending, twisting and folding the whole slab, we can begin to make three-dimensional abstract or representational forms. Some shapes will need to be supported in their new shape until they dry and harden.

Figure 64 *(opposite above left)*

Figure 65 *(opposite above right)*

Figure 66 *(opposite below left)*

Figure 67 *(opposite below right)*

Figure 68 *(above)*

Figure 69 *(below)*

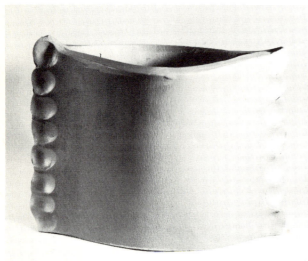

Figure 70 *(above)*

Figure 71 *(below)*

Other shapes will need to be constructed from a number of slabs. By pinching the edges of two slabs together, we can make a simple pot. To ensure a good join, the clay should be fairly soft. And tall forms can be made by curling the clay around itself.

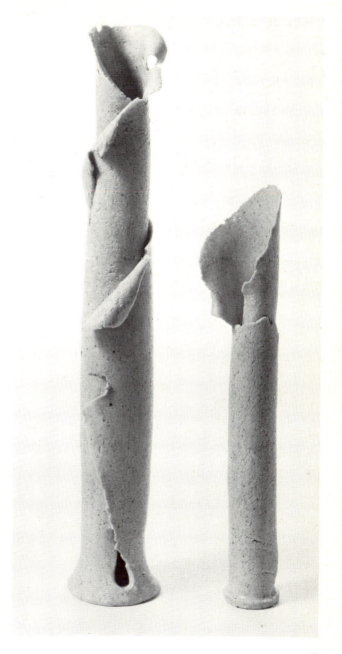

Figure 72   Tall, curled, sprouting forms by Mary Rogers

Figure 73 Pinching up the edge of the slab to make a simple dish

Next, we can use a rolled-out slab to make a simple dish. To make a deeper dish or bowl, the clay must be supported in some way, either in a convex or concave mould. Ready-made plaster moulds can be purchased directly from a pottery supplier, but it is cheaper and more creative to make your own.

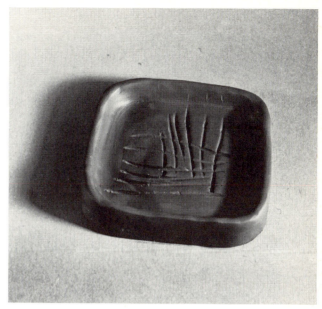

Figure 74 *(above right)* Adding a coil of clay around the edge

Figure 75 *(below left)* Adding a thin strip cut from the slab

Figure 76 *(below right)* Cutting the slab into a shape which can be folded in

CONCAVE MOULDS

One of the simplest ways is to rest the soft clay slab in a supporting coil of clay. When the dish hardens sufficiently to retain its shape, it can be taken out and finished-off by smoothing and decorating.

Larger dishes can be supported in a bed of soil or sand.

Figure 77 *(above right)*

Figure 78 *(below left)*

Figure 79 *(below right)*

Figure 80

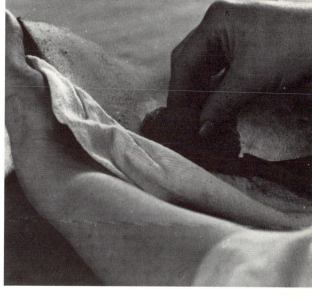

Figure 81

Next we can utilise a whole range of objects which are themselves concave in shape. A tin foil pastry case, cardboard boxes, bowls, plates, saucers, and dishes. To ensure that the clay does not stick to the inside of the mould, leave the clay on its rolling sheet of cloth or thin paper, and press them into the mould together.

1 Roll out a sheet of clay slightly larger than the mould for which it is intended. In this case, a metal casserole cover.

2 Gently and gradually press the clay, (still on its rolling cloth), into the mould. A damp sponge is useful for this.

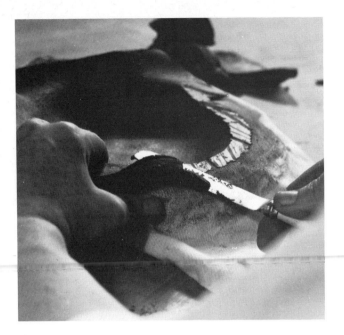

Figure 82

Figure 83

3   The excess clay, (whilst still soft), should be cut off with a knife. Take care, whilst cutting, to hold the clay in the mould, lest it is pulled out as it sticks to the knife.
4   Smooth-off the completed dish with a damp sponge.

When the clay hardens, it can be taken out, and the mould used again. The paper or cloth on which the clay was rolled-out can easily be pulled off, and the unfinished rim of the dish carefully smoothed-off. The support which a concave mould gives to the soft clay, makes it an excellent surface on which to decorate the dish by impressing, applying clay, or using liquid slips.

Figure 84

CONVEX MOULDS

In theory, most of the concave moulds, (dishes, etc), could be upturned and used as convex moulds, but it is much easier to use a heap of sand or a stuffed paper bag.

Here the slab is cut to the desired shape and draped over the mould until the clay hardens slightly, when it can be removed and finished. Finally, we can use clay slabs, fastened together, to make a wide variety of three-dimensional forms.

Figure 85

In order to illustrate the technique of fastening two pieces of slab together, let us suppose that we are to make a simple round pot.

Firstly, we must cut out a circular piece for the base, and a long narrow strip for the side. For the base, mark the outline with a suitably-sized round object, a lid or basin, and cut out the shape with a table knife, taking care to hold the knife vertically. Secondly, the edges to be fastened together must be scored, (not too deeply), with a modelling tool, (a matchstick or an old comb will do), and painted with thick slip (made from the same clay). If the clay is very soft, it can be fastened together quite securely without scoring and slipping. Thirdly, the two pieces are pressed very firmly together, the joins being carefully smoothed over with a modelling tool.

Figure 86 *(opposite above left)*

Figure 87 *(opposite above right)*

Figure 88 *(opposite below left)*

Figure 89 *(opposite below right)*

Figure 90

Figure 91 Slab bottle with incised decoration by Susan Luing

A tall round pot with an added coil top may need to be supported when first fashioning the shape, by building the clay around a tube of cardboard. Take care to remove the tube as soon as possible, to prevent the clay from shrinking and cracking.

Slab pots can be used as a base to be added to with other clay-working techniques, like this coil-extended container. They can be decorated in all kinds of ways. Numbers of slabs can be used together to make almost any kind of shape.

Figure 92 Silver lustre, oxidised stoneware by Tony Hepburn

Figure 93 *Garden*, ash/clay stoneware by Bryan Newman

Figure 94 Clay castle, African. Courtesy of the Trustees, British Museum

Figure 95 Pair of seagulls by Henrik Allert

Figure 96 Model farm, Chinese, Victoria and Albert Museum, Crown Copyright

6 MODELLING

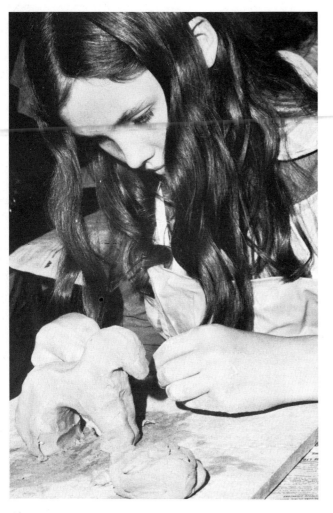

It would be wrong to hive off modelling as an activity distinct from pinch pottery, coiling, or slabwork. The fact that we do so in this book is for the convenience of illustrating the vagaries of specific techniques. In practice, they are very much interrelated; the activities of pinching, rolling, pressing, etc, which a young child discovers naturally as part of his early involvement with clay, making a positive contribution to the skills which will later be needed in making a pinch pot or a coil jar.

As previous chapters have shown, much that we might describe as 'modelling', (ie making a figure or an animal, as opposed to making a vase or a dish), necessarily involves the mastery of a specific, clay-working technique, and for that reason, modelling which makes use of these techniques have been excluded here. But this is an arbitrary distinction of convenience.

For the moment, we will consider some of the ways in which the young child's 'natural' handling of clay can be furthered and explored.

Firstly, by encouraging the manipulation of a single piece of clay with fingers and simple tools.

Figure 97

Figure 98   Shapes made by pinching

Figure 99   Simple shapes made by pulling out the clay

Figure 100   Shapes made by patting and beating

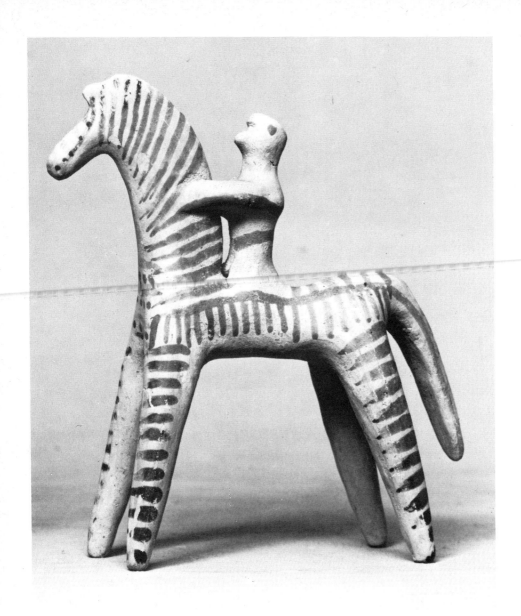

Figure 101 Pulled-out shape. Early Greek horse and rider. Courtesy of the Trustees, British Museum

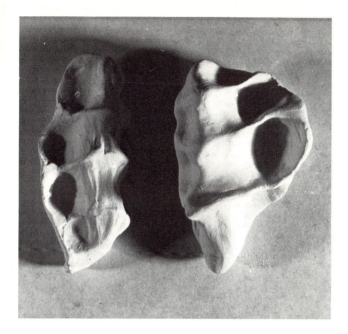

Figure 102 *(above left)*   Shapes made by squeezing clay

Figure 103 *(above right)*   Simple shapes made by shaping and smoothing with hands and fingers

Figure 104 *(below left)*   Pulling and pressing out the clay

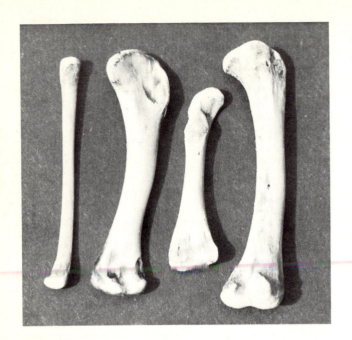
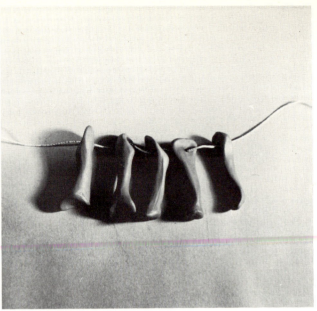

Figure 105 *(above left)*   Bones provide an excellent source of inspiration

Figure 106 *(above right)*   Bone-inspired pendant necklace

Figure 107 *(below left)*   Pebble-inspired hollow shape

Figure 108   Simple hollowed-out shapes

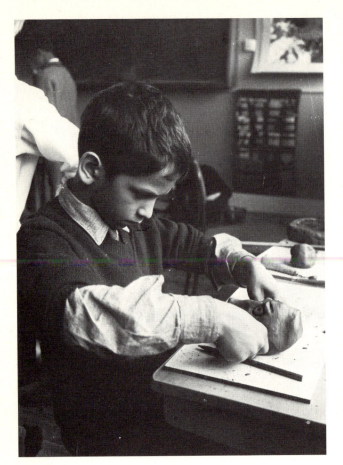

Figure 109   Making a clay head

Figure 110

Figure 111 *(above left)*   Cutting

Figure 112 *(above right)*   Bending

Figure 113 *(below right)*   Twisting

Figure 114

Secondly, by encouraging the use of 'amalgams' of clay pieces, rolls, pellets, etc; a natural enough technique which young children discover as a matter of course, in their first attempts at a basket of fruit, or a simple animal, but one to be fostered in all kinds of ways.

Figure 115 *(opposite above left)* Experimenting with rolls of clay

Figure 116 *(opposite above right)* Designing with coils

Figure 117 *(opposite below)* Experimenting with pellets of clay

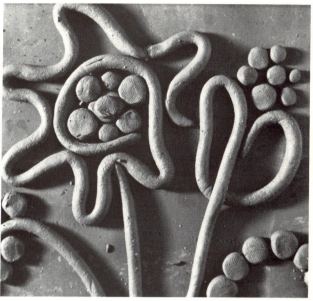

Figure 118 Simple beads

Figure 119 Using pellets of clay. A lion by Fernando Abranches

Figure 120 Clay dragon

Figure 121　Clay figures

Figure 122　*Penguin* by a pupil of Jan Colley

Figure 123 *(opposite)*　Glazed monkey, English eighteenth century, Victoria and Albert Museum, Crown Copyright

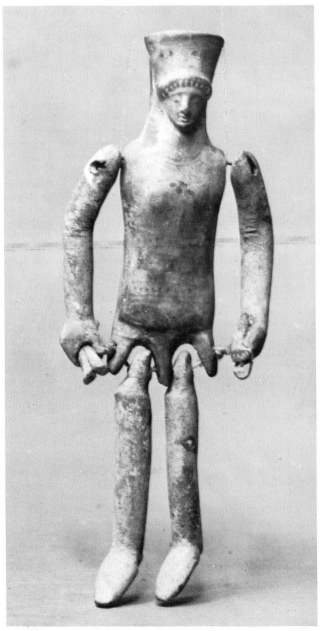

Figure 124 *(left)* Kneading bread, early Greek. Courtesy of the Trustees, British Museum

Figure 125 *(right)* Jointed doll, early Greek. Courtesy of the Trustees, British Museum

7 DECORATION

We usually think of the making of a pot and the decorating of a pot as two separate activities. In a sense, this is often the case, for it might be weeks or even months before the bare clay shape receives its final coat of glaze or surface decoration. Conversely there are times when the decoration of a pot is achieved as a direct result of the way in which the pot was made, when the process of making, and the process of decorating are indeed one and the same.

The decorative edging around the rim of a north American birchbark basket springs not from a desire to decorate an otherwise complete and usable form, but from the purely technical considerations involved in shaping the materials themselves. The mouth of a birchbark basket must be strengthened with a wooden hoop sewn around the rim. If the stitches were of equal length, they would each pass through the same grain of the bark wall, (for the grain of the bark runs parallel to the rim), and the whole rim would tear off. The resultant 'decorative' zig-zag pattern is formed by the technical necessity of making the holding stitches of different length.

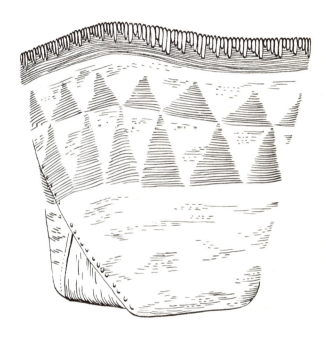

Figure 126

Figure 127 Beaker and pots, British, Bronze Age. Courtesy of the Trustees, British Museum

In contrast, the simple impressed and incised decoration of this early Bronze Age pot is decoration for its own sake. There is no technical necessity for decorating the pot in this way, or for decorating the pot at all.

It is highly probable that some of man's earliest vessels were clay-lined baskets, and equally probable that man's discovery of the clay-hardening property of fire stems from the accidental burning of such a basket. Not only would the burnt clay be stronger and more serviceable, it would also retain the impressions created when the soft clay was smeared around the inside of the woven basket. What more natural for primitive man, having grasped the significance of fire, to fashion future vessels from clay alone, and to retain the magic of their superior strength in the secret 'runes' which pattern their surface. In effect then, this decoration too, like the basket's rim, stemmed first from the way in which the article was made, rather than from man's penchant for decoration for its own sake.

But we should be careful not to make too rigid a distinction between decorative effects which are created as a result of the natural handling and shaping of the material, and decorative effects which are intentionally imposed. In pottery, both effects play their part.

For the moment, let us look at some of the ways in which processes of handling and shaping, affect the surface aspect of clay. Although there may be no conscious desire to 'decorate', these processes do achieve surface textures and patterns which are, to a greater or lesser degree, 'decorative'.

Figure 128 *(above)*   Decorative effect achieved by modelling with the fingers

Figure 129 *(centre)*   Roughly-modelled coil pot surface

Figure 130 *(below)*   Coils joined neatly with the fingers

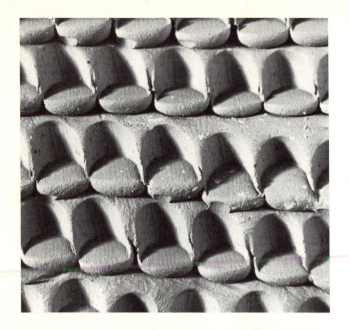

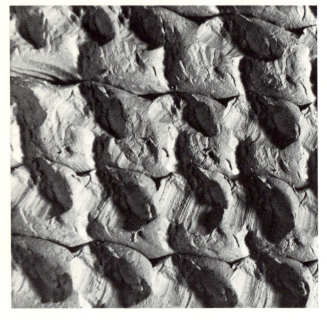

Figure 131 *(above)*   Coils joined with a stick

Figure 132 *(below)*   Coils joined with a pebble

Firstly, when the clay is in its soft, plastic state, it can be shaped by smoothing and pressing with the fingers or tools. (At this stage, the clay should never be over-wetted, since too much water will weaken the clay.)

Secondly, in its cheese-hard state, the clay can be successfully beaten, cut, and scraped. Too soft, and the beating instrument will stick-to and 'pull' at the shape. Too hard, and the surface aspect will be unaffected, or the entire shape sustain structural damage.

Beating is usually carried out with a fairly solid length of wood, about 15 mm ($\frac{1}{2}$ in.) thick, but one can experiment with all manner of things. Pieces of brick or slate, large pebbles, the back of an old shoe or clothes brush, and so on. More decorative effects can be achieved with a naturally textured instrument like a worn piece of wood, or pitted stone; or an artificially textured object like a piece of wood wrapped with string, or stuck with drawing pins.

Thirdly, in its hard, dry state, the clay can be scraped, scored or rubbed smooth.

Figure 133 *(opposite above left)*   Pebble-beaten surface

Figure 134 *(opposite above right)*   Stick (wrapped with string) beaten surface

Figure 135 *(opposite centre left)*   File-beaten surface

Figure 136 *(opposite centre right)*   Brush-beaten surface

Figure 137 *(opposite below left)*   Scoring the dry surface with an old saw blade

Figure 138 *(opposite below right)*   Scoring the surface with a wire brush

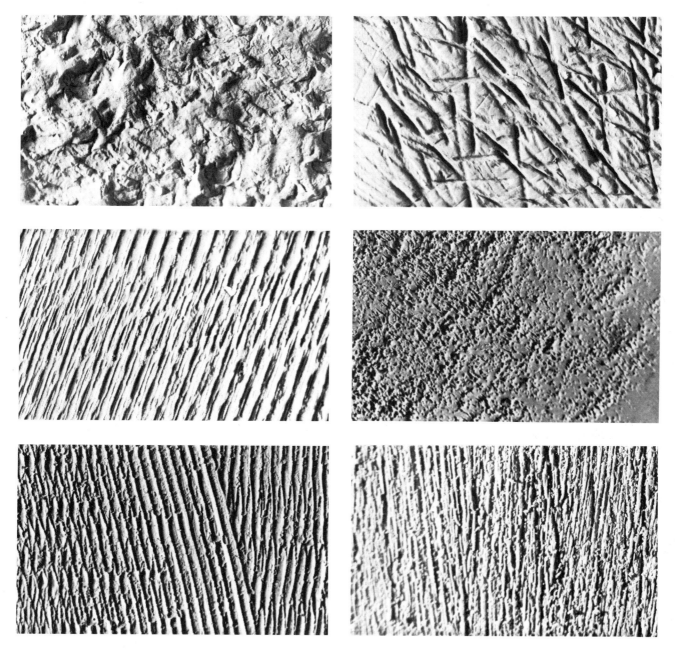

Figure 139 Fluting. Chinese earthenware jar, Victoria and Albert Museum, Crown Copyright

Figure 140 Burnished coil pot by Susan Luing

Finally, in a hard state, midway between cheese-hard and dry, the clay can be *burnished*. Primitive potters employ various techniques, some quite complex. The most satisfactory method for young children consists in polishing the clay with a smooth pebble or shell, or the back of a spoon. With small circular movements, the clay is pressed densely together achieving a highly-polished, glass-like effect. Clay to be burnished should preferably be free from sand or grog.

As the clay dries out, and if it is later fired, the glass-like polish will dull, but usually be reburnished to its former brilliance.

We now turn to decorative techniques intentionally applied. Although the techniques are here treated separately, in practice, any number of them might be used on the same pot or in conjunction with the shaping techniques described above.

83

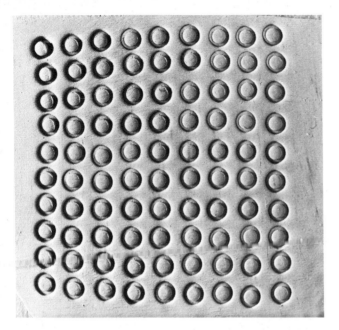

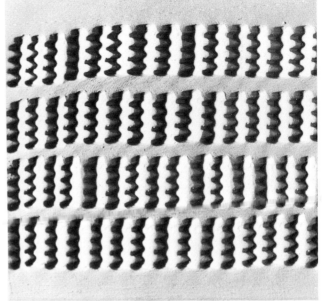

Figure 141 *(above left)*   Regular impressed design using a hollow tube

Figure 142 *(above right)*   Using a modelling tool

Figure 143 *(below left)*

IMPRESSING

Impressing is perhaps the simplest and most natural of all decorative processes, and can be effectively introduced by encouraging young children to experiment with the variety of effects which can be achieved by pressing small objects into plastic clay.

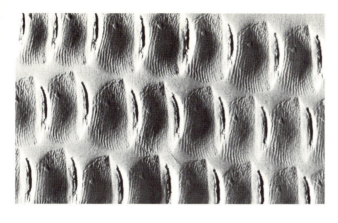
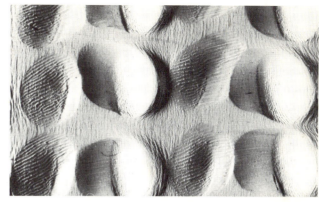
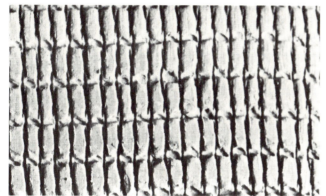

Figure 144 *(above left)*   Finger impressions

Figure 145 *(above right)*   Finger impressions

Figure 146 *(centre left)*   Open mesh fabric

Figure 147 *(centre right)*   String

Figure 148 *(below right)*   Wire loops

Figure 149 *(above left)*   Flowers

Figure 150 *(above right)*   Feathers

Figure 151 *(below left)*   Impressed tile

Some impressed effects are achieved by 'rolling' objects into clay; by patting and beating, or by pressing the clay itself into textured surfaces or materials.

Figure 152 *(above right)* Serrated bottle top, rolled across clay

Figure 153 *(below left)* Clay pressed into wood

Figure 154 *(below right)* Clay pressed into gravel

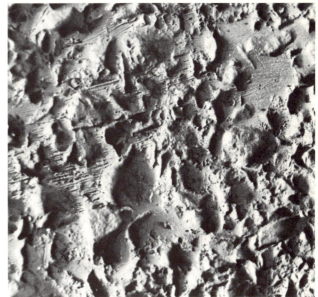

Figure 155 Tomb tile, Chinese fifth-sixth century AD, Gulbenkian Museum of Oriental Art, Durham

This decorative tile was produced by pressing the soft clay into a negative mould. Similar effects could be achieved by pressing clay into everyday objects; manhole covers, grids, cast iron signs, or old lino-cut designs.

Figure 156 *(above left)*

Figure 157 *(above right)*   Clay pressed into an old lino-cut

Figure 158 *(below right)*

Impressing is usually carried out directly onto the surface of a finished pot, but in dish making and slab work, the design may be impressed whilst the clay is in sheet form, and before the final shape is constructed.

APPLIED

Applied or relief decoration, where small pieces of clay are pressed onto the surface of a pot, is usually carried out whilst the clay is soft. It is important that the piece to be pressed on, and the pot itself, are of equal softness, and that the applied clay be firmly secured. If these conditions are not met, the applied clay will drop off as the pot dries. Unless the clay is very soft, and in all cases where the clay is cheese-hard, it is advisable to score and paint with slip, the faces to be joined together. (See overleaf.)

Figure 159 *(opposite above left)*

Figure 160 *(opposite above right)* Rolling the clay with a patterned roller

Figure 161 *(opposite below left)* Rolling netting into the clay

Figure 162 *(opposite below right)*

Figure 163 Applied decoration. German jug, Victoria and Albert Museum, Crown Copyright

Figure 164 *(above left)*   Using pellets

Figure 165 *(above right)*   Using coils

Figure 166 *(below left)*   Using pellets

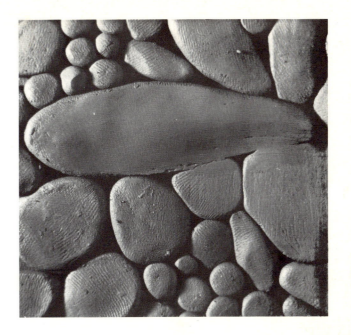

Figure 167 *(above left)*   Using coils

Figure 168 *(above right)*   Using clay shapes

Figure 169 *(below right)*   Using cut shapes

93

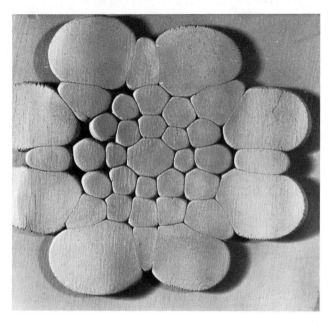

Figure 170 Rolling over pellets

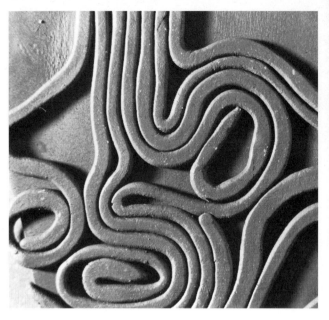

Figure 171 Rolling over coils

Finally, (and this applies particularly to the making of tiles, or in the preparation of sheets of clay for slab work or dish making), experiment with the effects which can be achieved by pressing down or rolling over the shapes which have been applied.

Figure 172 *(opposite)* Decorative panel, using rolled-over pellets and coils

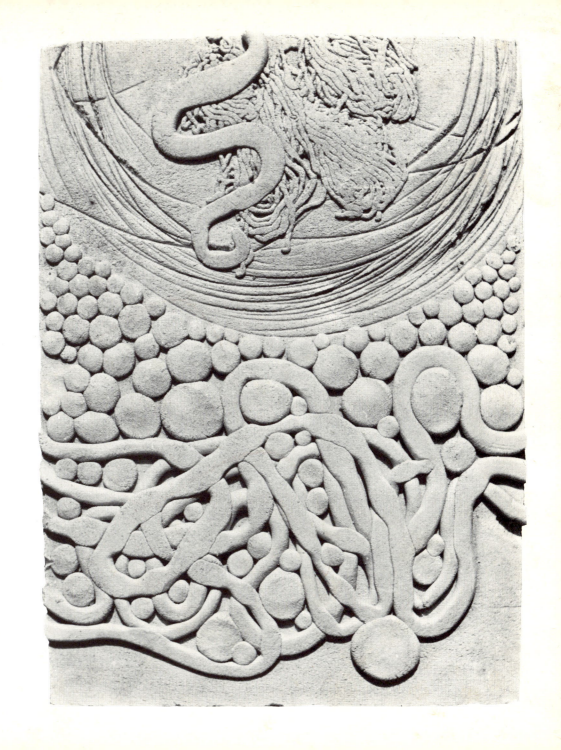

INCISED

There are a number of ways in which clay can be incised or engraved, but in general, the final effect depends on the tools employed, and the state of the clay. For most processes, the clay should be midway between cheese-hard and dry. Too soft, and the clay will pull and drag; too hard, and it will chip or flake. To begin with, experiment with simple tools which can be used for scratching and scoring.

Figure 173

Figure 174 Using a nail

Next, experiment with tools for combing.

Finally, experiment with tools which will cut and groove. Lino cutters make ideal tools for this.

Figure 175 Using an old saw blade

Figure 176 Using a lino cutter

Figure 177 Aztec pot with carved decoration. Horniman Museum, London

CARVING

This, in a sense, is an extension of incising, where the parts to be cut away are deeper and more pronounced. Any simple tools can be used; old knives, spoons, pieces of slate or metal, lino cutters, etc. It is best carried out whilst the clay is cheese-hard.

Figure 178　Carved bird panel

Figure 179　A pot carved through completely

Figure 180 Inlaid decoration. Flask from Cyprus, 2000 BC. Courtesy of the Trustees, British Museum

INLAY

The shapes produced by carving or incising can later be filled-in or inlaid with slip or paint of a different colour. The area to be inlaid should be brushed over with colour, (taking care that fine incisions are properly filled in), and allowed to dry. All excess surface colour can be scraped off with a knife, leaving the inlaid portions intact.

Figure 181 *(above right)*

Figure 182 *(below left)*

Figure 183 *(below right)*

PAINTED

With young children, (where it is not intended that the finished work be fired), painting can be carried out on the surface of a dry pot in exactly the same way that one would paint on a sheet of paper. The advantage of painting on dry clay is that the paint, (water paint, that is), will dry out in seconds. One could paint onto soft clay, but it would take longer to dry. Any kind of paint can be used, (watercolour, poster paint, powder colour, etc), even, if desired, oil-bound household paint or lacquer. Care should be taken when painting small, thin articles with water-based paint, since if the clay becomes too wet, too quickly, it is liable to disintegrate.

Drawing instruments, too, can be used, exactly as one would use them on paper. Pencil, pen and ink, crayon, pastel, chalk, felt pen, etc. Candles or wax crayons can be used as a resist before painting with water-based paint. And with all these materials, if anything goes wrong, or if the child wishes to start again, the applied colour can easily be scraped-off with a knife, or scoured-off with sandpaper or wire wool.

With the exception of oil-bound paints, the colouring matter will have no adverse effect on the clay itself, and unwanted models, paint and all, can be reconstituted as we described earlier.

For pottery which is to be fired, none of these methods is suitable, for with firing, any of the above colours would be burnt away. We will have more to say about colours used for firing in the following chapter.

Figure 185   Pencil drawing on clay

Figure 184 *(opposite)*   Plovers over waves. Painted Japanese dish, early eighteenth century, Cleveland Museum of Art, USA. Purchased from the J H Wade Fund

Figure 186 Painted dish by Pablo Picasso. Victoria and Albert Museum, Crown Copyright

Figure 187 *(opposite)* Dish with sgraffito design, Byzantine fourteenth century, Victoria and Albert Museum, Crown Copyright

SGRAFFITO

A method of scratching through a layer of paint or slip, to allow the colour of the clay body to show through.

Figure 188 Sgraffito bird by a six-year-old boy

Figure 189 *(opposite)* Dish with sgraffito design, English seventeenth century, Victoria and Albert Museum, Crown Copyright

Figure 190   Pouring in the slip

Figure 191   Covering the inside of the dish

SLIP DECORATION

Although most of the various methods of using slip are comparatively simple, even for young children, the use of slip decoration as a whole does present the teacher with a number of problems. Firstly, the problem of preparing, storing and handling the slip itself. Secondly, the practical problems involved in actually using the slip in a crowded classroom. And thirdly, the problem of keeping the finished pots out of harm's way during the often lengthy process of drying out. Given that these problems can be overcome, the use of slip decoration can be a rewarding and exciting experience.

Except in those circumstances where slip is being used as a colourant on dry clay, (as one would use paint), all slip techniques are carried out whilst the pot is midway between plastic and cheese-hard. Further, since such clay will become softer and weaker after its treatment with slip, the articles to be decorated should be fairly thick and substantial. Shallow bowls and dishes should be supported with a ring of clay, or in a bed of sand. To illustrate the various processes, we will assume that the article to be treated is a shallow pinch bowl.

1   The inside of the bowl is given a layer of slip by pouring in a small quantity of 'double-cream thick' slip, tilting the bowl carefully so that the slip moves towards the lip, and gently turning the bowl until the whole area is covered. Any excess slip can be poured off, and the lip wiped clean with a damp sponge. Simple stencil techniques can be effected by first covering the inside of the bowl with thin, paper cut-outs, wool, string, or wide-meshed fabrics. After slipping, (allowing time for the slip to harden slightly), the stencil can be removed.

2   Assuming that the bowl and the slip are made from differently coloured clays, the slipped bowl can be left to dry out, and later decorated with sgraffito designs.

3   Other slip techniques are carried out immediately after the bowl has been slipped, whilst the slip is still wet.

Figure 192 *(overleaf)*   Staffordshire slipware dish, seventeenth century, Victoria and Albert Museum, Crown Copyright

Marbling

We now need to apply the slip using a *slip trailer*. Trailers of various kinds can be bought from pottery suppliers, but for children, the plastic bottle variety with screw-on nozzle is the easiest to use.

Using a full trailer, slip can be applied in two ways. Either by pressing out small globules of slip; or by pressing out a steady stream from the lip of the bowl, allowing it to flow naturally into a trail. Great care must be taken to hold the end of the nozzle as close as possible to the slipped surface, without actually touching it. If the nozzle is too far away, the applied slip will splatter.

The marbling process is carried out whilst both slips are in liquid form, by tilting or swirling the bowl, and allowing the slips to run together. But be careful not to overdo it. Excessive tilting and swirling will mix the slips together into a formless mass.

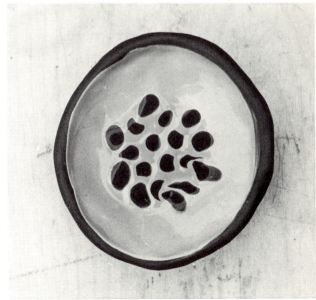

Figure 193 *(above)*   Slip trailer

Figure 194 *(below)*   Applying blobs of slip to a slipped dish

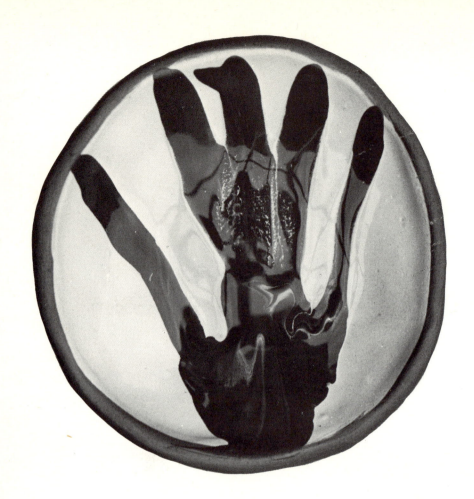

Figure 195 Applying trails of slip

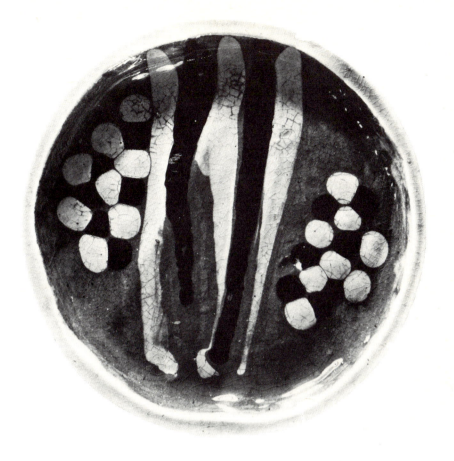

Trailing
In essence, slip trailing is carried out in the same way that one would pipe out icing onto a cake. Here too, great care must be taken not to touch the slipped surface with the end of the nozzle, nor to hold the nozzle too far away. This is a difficult art, and requires much practise. Children might best begin by experimenting with blobs of clay. Lines can come later.

Figure 196

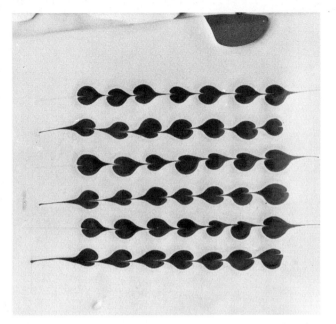

Figure 197

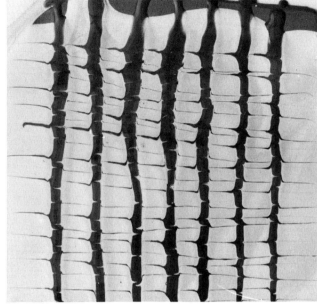

Figure 198

Feathering
Feathering consists in very delicately pulling or dragging through two colours of slip with a pin, a short length of fuse wire, or (of course), a sharply-pointed quill.

8 KILNS AND FIRING

To fire or not to fire. For the average teacher in the average primary school, it is hardly a fair question. It is not a case of whether clay needs to be fired, or whether clay ought to be fired, but a simple issue of whether or not it is physically possible to fire. It would be ideal if every school had a kiln, and every teacher could use one. Certainly it would provide children with more opportunities and more varied experiences. Nevertheless, although the provision of kilns in schools is on the increase, the possession of a kiln is itself no guarantee that the children who enjoy its use will come to understand and appreciate clay more deeply or more sensibly than those without it. Using clay can be a vital experience not because whatever one makes will eventually be burnt hard with fire, but because one is learning to come to terms with a material which comes alive when we hold it in our hands.

It is no small benefit to know that when we achieve something of worth, it can be given a lasting strength and permanence. And it is an advantage to be able to enhance the work with a fine glaze. But if this is not possible, it does not detract from the work that has gone before. Since many who use this book will be anxious to experiment with clay as a creative medium, yet be without access to a commercial pottery kiln, this chapter will be in two parts.

Figure 199 Childs clay basket

Figure 200

Figure 201

Firstly, concerning the construction of simple homemade kilns, together with some of the alternatives to firing. Secondly, concerning firing and glazing with a commercial kiln.

In situations where it is not possible to fire, clay models can be strengthened by varnishing. This should be carried out when the models are completely dry. Any kind of PVA adhesive, (this is the thick, white, treacly adhesive commonly used in schools), can be used, diluted with a little water. On first application, the PVA adhesive will appear rather cloudy, seeming to obliterate any painted decoration underneath, but as it dries, it clears to a shiny, transparent film. If the first coat remains dull, the process can be repeated. In practice, any other varnish, (household varnish, shellac, etc), can also be used.

One great advantage of this method is that clay can be used in conjunction with other materials; materials which, with firing, would be burnt away. Paper, card, feathers, sticks, leaves, wool, string, etc; indeed, any of the materials normally used for model making in the primary school.

KILNS AND FIRING

Although it is neither absolutely necessary, nor, in many cases, practicably possible to fire everything which children make from clay, it would be unreasonable to reject or ignore the process of firing out of hand.

Every effort should certainly be made to provide children with the experience of making and firing their own kiln. It is a uniquely rewarding experience which gives added dimension to the child's understanding of clay as a whole.

Indeed, since the firing techniques which I will now describe, are all relatively simple, and might reasonably be undertaken with infants, it should be possible for even the most hard-pressed teacher to provide her class with at least a taste of what kilns and firing are all about.

Man's first kiln was an open fire. A simple fire of wood, peat or straw, in which pots would be burnt hard. As a firing method, it has much to commend it, (it is, in fact, still used today in various parts of the world), and a primitive kiln of this kind would be an excellent starting point for work with young children. So where do we begin? Firstly, with the clay articles themselves. These should be fairly simple, thickly-made shapes, (pinch pots or small tiles might be best to begin with), of clay which has been mixed with sand or grog, to withstand any sudden changes in temperature.

On completion, the shapes must be left to dry out completely. The traditional test for dryness is to press the clay to one's cheek. If it feels warm, it is dry; if cold, it still contains traces of moisture. Not until the pots are completely dry, are they ready for firing.

Next, the kiln site. Any spare ground will do, suitably distant from surrounding buildings. Since smoke may be a hazard, check which way the wind is blowing.

For kiln fuel, collect firewood, twigs, wood shavings, sawdust etc. Quantities will depend on the size of the kiln, but do ensure that all fuels are completely dry.

Lay a foundation of twigs and shavings to form the 'floor' of the kiln. If the ground is wet, or the soil damp, 'fire' the site before you begin. Cover this foundation with a thick layer 50 mm to 100 mm (2 to 4 in.) of sawdust.

The first layer of pots, (themselves filled with sawdust), can now be placed in the sawdust bed, about 50 mm (2 in.) apart. Never allow pots to touch each other, nor place pots too near the edge of the foundation. Successive layers of pots are then built up, pyramid-style, to form a mound; each layer of pots interspersed with a layer of sawdust.

Finally, the whole mound is given a thick covering of sawdust, then shavings, twigs and firewood.

The function of the foundation and outer layer of shavings and twigs is to ignite the sawdust. The wood will burn fiercely for ten minutes or so, then die. The sawdust, when properly alight, will smoulder gently for a considerable time.

The increase in temperature is gradual inside the kiln. This is vital. Were the pots subjected to the sudden heat of burning wood, many would explode. With a slow-burning, protective covering of sawdust, this will not happen.

Figure 202 *(above left)*

Figure 203 *(above right)*

Figure 204

Figure 205

Figure 206 The finished pots, fired and cleaned

As the sawdust burns away, exposing the half-burnt pots, they can gently be pushed back and more sawdust added. No other stoking is necessary. In fact, it is best to leave the kiln altogether until it is completely burnt out. Actual firing time will be from twelve to twenty-four hours, depending on the size of the kiln. The one here was completely burnt away in twelve hours. Two hours after that, the pots were cool enough to be removed by hand.

The fired pots should be brushed or washed clean.

The essence of these home-made sawdust kilns is their simplicity. They provide us with a very cheap and very effective method of illustrating the clay-hardening property of fire.

Although it is possible to build bigger and more sophisticated kilns, few of them, if any, are practical possibilities for the classroom teacher. For those who do wish to perservere, the bibliography suggests a number of books in which these more sophisticated kilns are fully described.

Figure 207 *(above)* Similar firings can be carried out by using a metal drum pierced with holes. The drum is filled completely with *dry* sawdust with the articles dispersed throughout. A small fire-lighter placed on top of the sawdust will provide sufficient ignition. The fire should smoulder gradually downwards, without further attention

Figure 208 *(below)* Larger kilns can be made with housebricks put together like this. The firing procedure is exactly the same

Commercial kilns

For school work, a small electric kiln would be the most suitable means of firing children's work. Many different types and sizes are available, although their construction and operation are basically similar. Most suppliers have an advisory staff to meet the need for information regarding kiln placing, wiring and installation and possible fire risk.

Where costs are prohibitive, discuss the possibility of sharing a kiln with the local education authority and other local schools. Indeed, some schools may have a kiln which is no longer used and this may be re-sited.

Kiln firing

The firing of an electric kiln is no more difficult than the operation of a domestic oven. It is simply a matter of switching on and off; all kilns have regulators of one kind or another.

Rate of temperature increase

The firing of raw clay articles is called *biscuit firing*. Here it is important to effect a gradual increase in temperature (not more than 100°C per hour), up to about 500°C, to allow all the 'water' in the clay to be driven off. Even dry clay still retains 'water' which is not completely driven off until it reaches a temperature of between 350 and 500°C.

After this, the temperature increase can be rapid, up to the desired maturing temperature of between 900 and 1000°C. Most bought clays can be fired up to a temperature of 1200°C or more, but generally there is no necessity to go beyond 1000°C.

With the firing of glazed ware (which has been biscuited), the increase should be gradual for the first 100°C (to allow the evaporation of absorbed water), and may be rapid thereafter. The temperature required for glaze firing will depend on the glaze used. This is known as the *maturing temperature*.

Figure 209 A typical electric kiln. Courtesy of Wengers Ltd, Stoke-on-Trent

Temperature control
Cones Small, obelisk-shaped pieces of material, designed to melt and bend over at a given temperature. The cone is placed inside the kiln (in a ceramic holder or a pellet of clay, to hold the cone upright), opposite the spy-hole. When the cone bends over, the desired temperature has been reached and the kiln is switched off.
Pyrometers Heat-sensitive probes which protrude inside the firing chamber and record the internal temperature on an outside calibrated scale. In addition to these, there are a variety of other aids, designed not only to record the temperature, but to control the rate of increase of temperature, to control the input of power, and to switch the kiln off automatically when a desired temperature is reached. These are progressively more expensive.

Biscuit firing
As soon as the clay models are completely dry, they may be packed inside the kiln and fired. Where possible, flat, heavy objects should go at the bottom of the kiln. Two or three pots can be stacked inside each other, but take care not to impede the circulation of the air and avoid placing the models in contact with the elements. This operation is facilitated by building shelves of the desired height within the kiln.

On no account must the door of the kiln be opened whilst the electric current is switched on, or whilst the temperature is 100°C or more. During the gradual temperature increase up to 500°C, the spy-hole bung should be left out, after which it can be replaced.

Switch off when the desired temperature is reached. Allow the kiln to cool gradually until the models inside can be removed with bare hands. Under normal conditions, the maturing temperature of about 1000°C will have been reached in eight to twelve hours.

Figure 210 Kiln furniture used for shelf-building. The saddles *(middle shelf)* and the stilts *(bottom left)* support glazed articles during glaze firing. Courtesy of Wengers Ltd, Stoke-on-Trent

Glaze firing
Each model in glazed ware must be carefully packed in the kiln to provide a gap of about 15 mm ($\frac{1}{2}$ in.) between surrounding models or surfaces. The base of the model should be supported on a ceramic stilt. If this is not possible, the base of the model should be wiped free of glaze and placed on a little sand. If glaze is left on the base, it will become stuck to the support.

Kiln shelves should be painted with a solution of flint or *bat-wash* to protect them from drops of molten glaze which may run off the models where it has been too thickly applied, or the maturing temperature exceeded. After the initial drying-out period, (about one hour), with the spy hole bung left out, the bung can be replaced and the firing allowed to continue rapidly up to the desired temperature. Again, models must not be taken from the kiln until they are quite cool.

GLAZES AND COLOURANTS

A glaze is essentially a thin layer of glass covering the pottery article. Its purpose is practical, since a glazed pot is waterproof and easier to clean; also aesthetic, insofar that a glaze may enhance the appearance of a pot.

Where it is intended to use a glazed pot (a mug to drink from, or a dish to be eaten off), it is advisable to buy prepared glaze from a pottery supplier. Where this is not the case, it is cheaper and more exciting, to prepare one's own.

There are literally thousands of glaze recipes. There follows a very simple, cheap, highly reliable glaze, sufficient for most school needs. This is basically a transparent, earthenware glaze with a maturing temperature of 1080°C.

Ingredients
85 per cent lead bisilicate
15 per cent dry white clay

Method
Mix together 5·5 kilograms (8$\frac{1}{2}$ lb) of lead bisilicate in the form of a white power), or 1 kilogram (1$\frac{1}{2}$ lb) of dry white clay (any dry bits and pieces will do) with water. Make a solution the consistency of the 'top of the milk'. This makes about half a large bucketful of glaze. If the solution is lumpy it should be sieved; a fine kitchen sieve will do (but not to be used for cooking again), or a bought 120 mesh pottery sieve.

Figure 211 *(above left)*

Figure 212 *(above right)*

Figure 213

Figure 214

Figure 215

Application

This is done by dipping or pouring. The pots should be free from dust or greasy finger marks.

For dipping, hold the article between the finger and thumb, immerse into the previously-stirred glaze for two to three seconds; take out and allow to dry. The glaze will dry in seconds. Any unglazed parts should be dabbed over with the finger.

For pouring, the article may be hand-held, the glaze being poured over from a jug. If the article is very large and heavy, support it on sticks laid across a bucket or bin. The resultant film of powdered glaze should be about the thickness of a piece of matchbox cardboard. Should the glaze be too thin, it will appear dull and 'thin' after firing; too thick and it will run off the article during firing.

Much of the skill of dipping and assessing glaze thickness is a matter of experience alone, but where the glaze is obviously too thin or too thick, it can be washed off with water, the article allowed to dry and re-dipped.

With few exceptions, the foot or base of the article must be wiped clean of glaze with a wet sponge. If this is not done, the molten glaze will adhere to the ceramic stilt which supports the article during firing.

Ceramic colourants
The basic ceramic colourants are *metal oxides*. Oxides of iron, copper, cobalt and manganese, providing yellow-reds/browns, green, blue and purple-brown respectively. In practise, they can be mixed together to provide other colours. They can be used in three general ways.
As glaze colourants Although they can be added directly to the glaze mixture, pre-sieving through a fine 200 mesh sieve prevents excessive speckling.

Additions of metal oxide to the transparent glaze:
2–5 per cent iron oxide gives
light to dark amber/brown
2–4 per cent manganese oxide gives
light to medium purple-brown
1–3 per cent copper oxide gives
light to medium green
$\frac{1}{4}$–2 per cent cobalt oxide gives
light to dark blue

Glaze mixtures containing different types and quantities of oxides can be mixed together without ill effect.

Excessive amounts of copper oxide (5 per cent plus) will produce a pewter glaze effect. Excessive amounts of iron or manganese oxide (7 per cent plus) will produce rich browns and blacks.
As slip colourants The quantities to be added and the resultant colours, are roughly as above, but it is essential to use white or grey clay, and to mix in the oxide whilst the clay is in liquid form. The use of slips is described in chapter seven.
As direct colourants to be painted onto the clay article
Basically, the raw oxide is mixed with water and painted onto the surface of the clay article, before or after biscuit firing, or onto the glaze surface.

Assuming that the article is of white or grey clay, the colour and effect achieved is roughly the same, at whatever stage the oxide is applied. The oxides themselves are extremely strong (cobalt particularly so), and only a small amount mixed with water will produce a strong colour.

Again, experience is the only guide, but as a general rule, oxide solutions for painting onto clay should have the appearance of watered-down writing ink.

Note
Used sensibly, none of the materials involved are dangerous to children. Care should be taken not to introduce glazes or oxides into the mouth. Protective clothing should be worn and hands should be washed thoroughly after using glazes and oxides.

The attention of all teachers is drawn to the Administrative Memorandum Number 2/65 and also Number 517/55, issued by the Department of Education and Science, which refers to the regulation of chemical materials in schools.

BIBLIOGRAPHY

CARDEW MICHAEL *Pioneer Pottery* Longman, Harlow 1969
LEACH BERNARD *A Potter's Book* Faber, London 1940; distributed in the USA by Transatlantic Arts Inc, New York
BILLINGTON DORA *The Technique of Pottery* Batsford, London 1962
Classic books covering every aspect of the potter's art.

MARSHALL SYBIL *Experiment in Education* Cambridge University Press, London and New York (now reissued in paperback)
A classic account of life and work in the primary school.

ROBERTSON SEONAID *Beginning at the Beginning with Clay*
A pamphlet issued by the Society for Education Through Art. A sensitive introduction to using clay by a remarkable teacher.

Ideas on what to do and what to make in the classroom
SCHMITT-MENZEL ISOLDE *Fun with Clay* Batsford, London 1969; Van Nostrand Reinhold, New York
RÖTTGER ERNST *Creative Clay Craft* Batsford, London 1963; Van Nostrand Reinhold, New York
KAMPMANN LOTHAR *Clay Modelling* Batsford, London 1971; Van Nostrand Reinhold, New York
HARTUNG ROLF *Clay* Batsford, London 1972; Van Nostrand Reinhold, New York
COWLEY DAVID *Working with Clay and Plaster* Batsford, London 1972; Watson-Guptill, New York

Kilns and kiln making
RHODES DANIEL *Kilns: Design, Construction and Operation* Pitman, London 1968; Greenberg, New York
FRASER H *Kilns and Kiln Firing for the Craft Potter* Pitman, London 1969
BJORN A *Exploring Fire and Clay* Van Nostrand Reinhold, New York 1969
See also CARDEW above.

Appreciation of clay artifacts
RAWSON PHILIP *Ceramics* Oxford University Press, London 1971
Illustrations of pottery and clay constructions of all kinds.
CHARLESTON R J (ed) *World Ceramics* Hamlyn, London 1968
BIRKS ANTHONY *The Art of the Modern Potter* Country Life, London 1967
CASSON MICHAEL *Pottery in Britain Today* Tiranti, London 1967

SUPPLIERS

GREAT BRITAIN

There are a number of major firms who supply almost anything to do with clay and who are always ready to assist and advise on problems arising from the use of clay in school.

E J Arnold and Company Limited
(School Suppliers)
Butterley Street
Leeds
LS10 1AX
also kilns

The Fulham Pottery
210 New Kings Road
London SW6

Harrison Mayer Limited
Meir
Stoke on Trent
also lead bisilicate

Podmore and Sons Limited
Shelton
Stoke on Trent
Staffs

Watts Blake and Bearn Limited
Newton Abbot
Devon

Wengers Limited
Etruria Works
Stoke on Trent
Staffs

Clay
Moira Pottery Company Limited
Moira
Near Burton on Trent

Potclays Limited
Brick Kiln Lane
Etruria
Stoke on Trent
Staffs

Kilns
Allied Heat Company Limited
Electurn Works
Otherstool Way
Watford By-pass
Watford
Herts

British Ceramic Services Company Limited
Bricesco House
Wolstanton
Newcastle under Lyme
Staffs

Kilns and Furnaces Limited
Keele Street Works
Tunstall
Stoke on Trent
Staffs

USA

Most large art supply stores carry modeling clay. The following is a list of some of the major ceramic suppliers. A catalogue will be sent on request.

American Art Clay Co
4717 West 16th Street
Indianapolis, Indiana 46222

Cedar Heights Clay Co
50 Portsmouth Road
Oak Hill, Ohio 45656

Craftools Inc
401 Broadway
New York, NY 10543

Denver Fire Clay Co
3033 Black Street
Denver, Colorado

W H Fairchild
712 Centre Street
Freeland, Pennsylvania 18224

Newton Pottery Supply Co
Newton, Massachusetts

Stewart Clay Co Inc
133 Mulberry Street
New York, NY 10013

Western Ceramic Supply Co
1601 Howard Street
San Francisco, California 94103